102 Dad Jokes
Ready for Liftoff

DAD JOKES

LAUNCH STATION

A GIANT LEAP FOR DADKIND

JACK WEST

I always felt that a good Dad joke
is launched like a rocket, and it lands
with...an explosion of laughter, or a
thud, or both. These jokes will fit
the bill! You'll laugh, you'll cringe,
you'll bury your face in your hands.
I hope you enjoy this hand-crafted
collection of some of my original,
ludicrous and hilariously terrible
Dad jokes!

Ready for Launch?

Say Hi, and get other stuff here:

www.JackWest.net

1.
What's it called when you take a potato on a walk?

——————————▶

A tater trot.

2.
What's the best cheese in the world?

——————————▶

That's a gouda question.

3.

What is the werewolf's favorite movie?

———————————————➤

"When Hairy Met Sally".

4.

What do you call it when a thermometer throws a fit?

———————————————➤

A temperature tantrum.

5.
What did the Jedi say
to the cowboy?

——————————————▶

May the horse be with you.

6.
How do angels greet one another?

——————————————▶

"Halo."

7.
Why did the lawnmower need so much fuel?

——————————➤

It was a grass guzzler.

8.
What do you call hamburgers in space?

——————————➤

Meat-iorites.

9.
What do you call a snail riding a goat?

→

Escargoat.

10.
When did the chicken finish work?

→

5 o'cluck.

11.
Why didn't the cannon show up to work?

→

It was fired.

12.
What did the surprised carpet say?

→

I'm floored.

13.
How did the cat cut the grass?

→

With a lawn meow-er

14.
What happened to the old bullfrog?

→

He croaked.

15.
Why were the two ponies sent to detention?

———————➤

They were horsing around.

16.
Why did the percussionist feel out of place?

———————➤

He stood out like a sore drum.

17.
What's it called when a sheep hits a home run?

→

A grand lamb.

18.
Why was the guitar free?

→

There were no strings attached.

19.
Do you like insects?

→

They bug me.

20.
Why was the gardener overwhelmed?

→

She was in the weeds.

21.
Why is the furnace so healthy?

⟶

Because it's always running.

22.
How do kayakers watch TV?

⟶

They stream it.

23.
What's an iPhone's favorite thing to read?

———————————➤

The phone book.

24.
How do bank robbers organize their thoughts?

———————————➤

Bullet lists.

25.
What do you call somebody who fights evil with music?

➡️

A Guitar Hero.

26.
What do princesses grow in their gardens?

➡️

Uni-corn.

27.
What did the iPhone say to the wall calendar?

→

Your days are numbered.

28.
How do dogs stop music from playing?

→

They hit paws.

29.
What did the kitchen feel naked?

———————————————▶

It dropped its drawers.

30.
What did the baker say when his bread exploded?

———————————————▶

That's the yeast of my problems.

31.
Why is it so hard to get a room at the Library Hotel?

→

They're all booked.

32.
Who did Dorothy bring her lamb to see?

→

The Wizard of Baaas.

33.
What did the hot dog say to the hamburger?

———————————————▶

It's nice to meat you.

34.
Why was the log punished?

———————————————▶

It was knotty.

35.
How do skeletons blow their nose?

———————————▶

With muscle tissue.

36.
What did the goofy golfer
have for lunch?

———————————▶

A turkey club.

37.
Why do some golfers have binoculars?

➤

They love watching birdies.

38.
What's the most popular music in Antarctica?

➤

Southern Rock

39.
Why was the man always chasing things?

→

He had a runny nose.

40.
Why are coat hangers so relaxed?

→

They just hang around all day.

41.
Why was the chicken in jail?

→

It ran a-fowl of the law.

42.
What did the rabbit buy
his fiancee?

→

A ten carrot ring.

43.
Why did the Grizzly quit his job?

————————————▶

He just couldn't bear it.

44.
Why did the dragon sleep with the light on?

————————————▶

He was afraid of the knight.

45.
How do you check the width of a pancake?

→

Use a crepe measure.

46.
Why was the puppy excited for winter?

→

Because every dog has its sleigh.

47.
How did the pirate wear his patch-patch?

→

Over his aye-aye, matey.

48.
Why did the boat get married?

→

She loved her buoy-friend.

49.
How did the jazz musician bring her meals to work?

→

In her lunch sax.

50.
Why was the bald man never worried?

→

He didn't have a hair in the world.

51.
How come Santa couldn't find the right chimney?

———————————→

He was a lost Claus.

52.
Why did the sandwich need help?

———————————→

It was in over its spread.

53.
What is a corn chip's favorite dance?

➤

Salsa.

54.
Why was the baking flour grumpy?

➤

It broke up on the wrong side of the bread.

55.
What do you call a melon who wants a big wedding?

→

Can't-elope

56.
Why do people skydive in tandem?

→

They need a pair-of-chutes.

57.
Why was the tape measure terrified ?

➡

It was within an inch of its life.

58.
Why couldn't Gumby buy a bigger house?

➡

He didn't have enough dough.

59.
What's a psychic's favorite treat?

————————————➤

A Fortune cookie.

60.
Why are bakers no good
at carpentry?

————————————➤

They always hit the nail on the bread.

61.
Where do gardeners take their clothes?

➡

To the lawndry mat

62.
Why did the farmer buy so many baby chicks?

➡

They were cheep, cheep, cheep.

63.
Why did the scientist reinvent bagel toppings?

➡️

She wanted to think outside the lox.

64.
Why was the elderly pig so youthful?

➡️

It aged like a fine swine.

65.
Why was the bomb so ill-tempered?

→

It had a short fuse.

66.
What's better - a stepstool or a stepladder?

→

The latter.

67.
What bait do fishermen use for smart fish?

→

Bookworms.

68.
Why was the woman envious of Earl Grey?

→

It wasn't her cup of tea.

69.
Why did the dermatologist change her mind?

→

It was a rash decision

70.
Why are spice cabinets dangerous?

→

They're known for a-salt.

71.
Why was the soda frustrated?

→

It was all bottled up.

72.
What did the bisque say to the chowder passing on the street?

→

'Soup?

73.
What's a hobbit's favorite cookie?

→

Shortbread.

74.
Why are trees afraid
of the dentist?

→

Root canals.

75.
What do you call a shot of coffee in a hurry?

———————————————▶

Expresso.

76.
How was the mathematician saved by geometry?

———————————————▶

He found his guardian angle.

77.
**Why was the squirrel
so unsure of itself?**

———————————————▶

It was out on a limb.

78.
**Who won the dress up
competition?**

———————————————▶

It was a tie.

79.
Why was the cobbler confident he got the job?

————————➤

He was a shoe in.

80.
Why was the oyster so positive?

————————➤

It was happy as a clam.

81.
Why did the oyster suddenly stop talking?

→

It clammed up.

82.
Why was the bike so mean?

→

It was a vicious cycle.

83.
How do you silence a wine bottle?

→

Put a cork in it.

84.
What's the 1st thing boxers do at work?

→

They punch the clock.

85.
Why are chickens
such bad friends?

———————————➤

They egg you on.

86.
What's the best
flower to kiss?

———————————➤

Two-lips.

87.
How does a tailor take it easy on you?

→

He cuts you some slack.

88.
How does a fisherman take it easy on you?

→

He lets you off the hook.

89.
Why did the pelican have
a raspy voice?

————————————➤

He had a frog in his throat.

90.
What did the pancake
say to the pan?

————————————➤

Catch you on the flip side.

91.
Why did the confused puppy growl at the cheese?

———————————————➤

It was barking up the wrong brie.

92.
Why was the leprechaun such a good hockey player?

———————————————➤

He had the puck o' the Irish.

93.
What do stockings do when they're afraid?

→

They run.

94.
What happens when a chicken breaks a mirror?

→

7 years of bad cluck.

95.
What's the best way to pay for a new battery?

——————————————▶

Charge it.

96.
What did the athlete say to the barista?

——————————————▶

Just brew it.

97.
How did the cheeses come to an agreement?

→

They met each other half-whey.

98.
What did the axe do with the log?

→

They called it splits.

99.
How do you get a railroad job?

→

You have to be well trained.

100.
How do bakers make guacamole?

→

With avoca-dough.

101.
Why couldn't the
boardgame be trusted?

---------------------------➤

It had a checkered past.

102.
Did you hear about the
handsome librarian?

---------------------------➤

He's a good booking guy

That's it, hope you enjoyed the book, I'm working on the next one now - please sign up below and I'll let you know when the next one comes out - and free offers too!

www.jackwest.net

Made in the USA
Middletown, DE
24 May 2022

66016129R00033